Canvas

Apurba Chakraborty

Qurate
quratebooks.com

Canvas

First Edition: 2023

© Published by

Qurate Books Pvt. Ltd.
14, Acron Watervista, Carona
V.P. Aldona, North Goa
Goa 403523, India
www.quratebooks.com

ISBN:978-81-19263-40-0

Dedicated To

This book is dedicated to
all poetry lovers of the world.

Preface

Preface to the first edition

In this book, each poem is an expression & of feelings from the core of my heart and soul with the colorful experience in the passage of my life.

What I have seen on the way of my journey is presented as the voice in every individual poem with a different tune and rhythm.

Introduction

Dear Reader,

The first edition of ' Canvas' is being published. In this edition, I have presented from the long colorful journey of my own experience in the form of poems with Different tastes. I tried to present the language of poems in my composition. Your well wishes, inspiration, and affections are the only assets for me to Go ahead in the way of the direction of a successful end.

With Thanks & Regards,

The writer of Canvas

Apurba Chakraborty

Contents

01.

Canvas

Today the presence of members is very less in the lake club,
Only a handful of friends are sitting in the lounge.
In front of the lounge, the lake water flows quite
With small soundless waves.
The sound of the waves doesn't reach this bank of the lake club.
On the opposite bank, a picture of a silent water painting
Like a canvas of an unknown whimsical painter.
As far as visible on the opposite bank can be seen
Few old banyan trees and horse trees with some other unknown plants.
The canvas is yet to be filled with swans and ducks
Are also absent this afternoon.
Today only a few eagles are flying in the blue sky above the lake water.
They have also come to join us to take a breath in the open air.
Still, the canvas needs more so I have to come back again
As the painting is to be filled by an unknown whimsical painter

02.

This World Is One Country

The dream of world humanity and harmony is possible
Only that day when the whole world will be one country.
We used to identify ourselves as citizens by the names of different countries,
On the world map, all the countries are correctly marked.
We human beings are only marked rubbing the ink & pen.
When this world will be only mine?
There will be no passport and visa
And when there will be no limitation of borderline in the territory
When the dark night will be abolished from all borders by the new light of hope?
When we all can tell with the total right. like Mount Everest is mine
Similarly, for the Alps and Kumayun, we have the same right.
Like Ganges,Jamuna Saraswati,Narmada & Gdabari,Damodar today is mine.
Similarly, Mississippi, Rhine, Danube, Volga, Nile & Tames
Also, when shall be for us all?
When we have the equal right in the sky like the seasonal birds?
I shall fly from Antarctica and Siberia through Ethiopia and Germany via Russia
To Bharatpur of India.

03.

The New Born

The newborn baby who took birth this morning,
Announces his arrival by screaming sound.
His surroundings vibrate in the resonance of screaming
The newborn expresses his right with closed-fisted small hands.
He arrived today with the messenger of the new era.
The new sun of the morning spreads the blush in the east direction.
The new sun is spreading orange color in the sky.
The silk cotton and the flame of the forest of spring bloomed along the horizon.
And the cuckoo welcomes the newborn baby with a sweet melodious tune
On this earth which is beautiful and full of magical light.
This world celebrates the auspicious occasion of the arrival of the newborn baby.
And the newborn baby claims his right throwing his little legs and closed fists to the world
The newborn baby strongly announces the bright forthcoming future
And claims his own right.to mother earth, the mother obstetrician
And to his mother who carried her for nine months frequently.
At first, I welcome you, oh newborn you have taken birth just this happy morning.

04.

The Endless

The Ocean of life flows in the direction
On the way to endless infinity.
Don't know when the walk started on the road
That road was also lost and wiped off & smoky today.
Even though it is unknown we have to go ahead.
This is life and the Ocean of life knows to move only.
So it is the tradition to go ahead in a direction
Without any destination.
Up till today, the Ocean of life flows
Sometimes it's slow and sometimes fast.
It never stops for a moment even.
In this endless voyage sometimes
Life loudly laughs and dances by clapping in rhythm,
Sometimes drown in deep thinking when affectionate.
Everything ends when life lands on reality.
Although life has to proceed onwards
Towards the direction of infinity
Which is endless and unknown.

05.

The Sound of Footsteps

Listening to the very light sound of footsteps of history,
The sound of footsteps is relative to the present era.
That sound gets lost in due course of time,
Who knows in which black hole the sound vanishes?
Again later some time I listen to the future is arriving
Very slowly step by step in one auspicious moment.
The present stands sill astonished silently
In the midst of the past and future.
Only the sound of the very light footsteps
That whispers from the past.
In the dawn when the sun sets the sound of the ringing bell
Comes with the chanting of the evening prayer
From a temple very nearby.

06.

This Road

This road this endless road,
The roof of this road is the blue sky spread to the unlimited horizon.
The heart of this road is deep like the ocean.
Through this road, the legends arrived on this earth again and again.
Through the same road red eyed invaders attacked time and again.
During the last right, this road only guides the direction of the journey to heaven,
The way towards the endless infinity.
On this road, only the lovers sing the eternal song of love and affection
And they wish the walk through this road never finish.
The same road moves rush of processions to claim the human rights
For the movement the demand of the road.
Again this road gives shelter who are helpless and who are in nowhere.
This road never gets tired.
Everybody irrespective of caste and creed has a great dependence on this road.
When your own home throws out this road welcomes you affectionately in silence.
The sound of life and the cry of death with the dance of hope and despair all in this road.
The starting of civilization is on this road and this road is the witness of destruction also.
This road is the silent witness of history,
This road this road this road this road only.

07.

Why So

My heart beats suddenly for you I don't know why so,
The story is very old from my youth time.
You never looked at me in your eye gesture never for a while
I never mind all those days.
Even though I looked at you squinting when you passed through the lane
Crossed. me regularly avoiding me like a swan,
On the way to your music class like a fairy of my dream.
I remember a guitar in your hand emitting the buzz of Asavari.
I wait for you looking for your return and passing my time
With my friends just in the namesake of gossiping.
Time flows in its own course.
You will return in the late evening when the sun will set in the west.
You are the princess of my imagination now you are coming again
In the same way, creating a sensation and rhythmic movement
Agan you disappear in your own style.
Why so my heart beats you are not aware,
My sweet dream you an illusory imagination only.

08.

The Array Of Clouds

The hide-and-seek of the mountain with the array of clouds
Is like a romantic evergreen game of teasing in between them.
The array of clouds enjoys agile games sometimes it touches
The rough and tough heart of the mountain and sometimes
The array of clouds goes far away from the mountain.
Like a budding love affair get bonding between the two lovers.
Again sometimes the array of clouds avoids
The touch of the mountain & run away.
Suddenly the gust appears and warns the cloud
Oh, array these acts don't suit you your birth is in the ocean.
You are the daughter of the ocean and brought up in the sky
So I have the first right to on you and you are mine only.
The array of clouds doesn't listen to the wind.
She only roams around the mountain to get its affectionate touch
And roams again and again in romance with the rough mountain.

09.

They Kept Their Promise

Nobody keeps their promise but they have kept their promise to each other.

They mean Abir and Mohana who are neighbors.stays nearby
Abir's love was not successful. To be fulfilled with Mohana.
As Mohana is the elder daughter have a lot of responsibilities
She is a teacher in a government school and has four sisters & brothers.
Mohana's father is a retired person pension holder.
Abir is the only son of his parents.
This Abir and Mohana exchanged their hearts with each other.
Both of them made a promise to walk all through the life
Keeping the sky wind and the falling leaves as a silent witnesses.
Days passing they can't wait and stop like the fallen leaves.
Abir is busy with his routine office work Mohana also has no time
After fulfilling her responsibilities & commitments.
And all the other matters move as usual in the traditional way.
The time doesn't wait it moves with the time clock in its own way.
In the meantime, Abir & Mohana both attain white hair
They are now approaching near to fifty years by this time.
Still, these two are the same as they were in their twenty-five years of age
In their youthful youth.
In the mass of nobody keeps their word Abir & Mohana are different
So in these days, people are there who keep their word.
Like they kept their promise to each other.

10.

Searching For

Searching for my lost childhood and the call of greeneries
In the fried Yellow Pages of my past.
Searching for rhymes and fairy tales of the princess
Told by grandfather & mother and in those stories the prince
Flies in the blue sky on the horse with wings
In the attraction unknown direction of the magical palace
Where the princess is in deep sleep one side is a golden stick
And the other side is a silver stick which are secret to wake her.
Listening to these charming stories my innocent little childhood
Used to lose in deep sleep with dreams with excitement.
Searching for the cradle songs of my mother and sister
By the magic of which tunes slowly, I used to lose myself in a deep sleep.
Searching for that particular magical tune of that song with the lyrics
The moon is visible on the bush of bamboo trees which had a
Very simple and magical effect with spontaneous expression.
Searching for the excitement of my childhood full of dust
Of the narrow muddy lanes and my lost youth in the cemented lanes
Of the refugee colony and those days when it was a luxury
To watch a movie in the hall while sitting wooden chair
In the middle of the rear row and weave colorful dreams of imagination.
Searching for the girl whose movement is like a butterfly
And whose sweet smell intoxicated my blooming desperate youth.
Searching for those days after passing the higher secondary
When admitted to the college and tasted first cigarette smoke.
Searching for those days when I felt myself grown up and in the
Colorful youth time got the first appointment letter for joining
And got independent to fulfill my commitments and responsibilities.

Searching for those days to stand with the neiboughers hand in hand
In danger & in good and bad times with relatives. and sharing with them.
Searching for so many things but time knows only to flow like a river.
All the happy moments are memories in each dry yellow page of the life book.
Searching for the last time at the end of the day looking back
Once again with the setting sun on the western horizon
Before getting lost in the sharp bend of life.

11.

I'm In Love

I'm in love with you and love the smell of your body,
In the mid-summer smell of leaching sweat
And in the monsoon your desperate caress with a heavy shower.
Again before the sunset, my full body including each and every pore gets excited
Your sweet breeze and flash of a naughty smile
Intoxicate me in my hungry body and mind.
I get lost slowly.in your upward and downward slopes
On the night of chill winter with shivering cold by your touch.
At the end of spring when new leaves bloom in the attraction of your colorful love
I swim with my crazy love in your flowing affection.
Whenever I go to any other enthralled beautiful city in this world,
Maybe that city is far away in the country or maybe abroad a magical city.
I have to go there on time and again for the sake of so many reasons.
Although I'm in love with you and reach to take rest in your assured lap
Which is full of evergreen and exuberant ever youth nest of affection.
I take a breath full of my heart.
You always bear roaring waves with a beauty spot you my love.
Every time I separate from you I come nearer to you and love you always
As you are only mine & eternal nearest to my mind my own city alone.

12.

The Right

Who has donated the right and when?
Right, can not be given in donation.
Right means life and death
Right, have to be earned.
Right means the dance of destruction.
Against the direction of the flow.
Right means the movement is the result of the rebellion.
All the great revolutions all the glorious stories on this earth
Have the background bloodshed movements.
And narrates the painful history of a fight with the tyrant ruler.
Right from the movement of May Day in Chicago to the French Revolution
Till India's freedom movement, inspiration and energy is the word Right.
The right is for the labor, the farmer for the absorbed
And right is for not to bow down the head
Right is for humanity and for the oppressed mass.
Even today also they earn the right in lieu of blood only..

13.

Flute You Sing

The flute is lying silently in one corner in negligence,
Sometimes it sounds on its own by the flow of wind.
With the keyboard. mouth organ and many other unknown
Music instruments are there in the orchestra troop but they
Can not play like you flute.
Oh flute you sing in your own magnificent magical tune
Let your tune spread all over the world's culture.
Let the peacock's wings and the snake hood dance
Let the lightning flash on the array of clouds all around. the horizon.
You sing oh flute synchronizing the bandish meghmallar
Or in raga Basantbahar so that the creation will enjoy your magical melody.
Don't know the direction of the deepest mind so, please
Don't sing the tune of Behang in this odd situation.
In this late hour oh flute all are eager to listen to your joyous tune
Oh flute you sing loudly and distribute happiness all around..

14.

In Search of Poem

The poets search for their poems in the lane and fields
On the hilltop, mountain caves in the forests & green bushes
If they couldn't found then they search for poems
In the deep ups and downs of a woman's body
He searches like a mad drunken man.
My poems are swimming in the open sky in the
Affectionately in love with the direction of the wind.
Sometimes my poems swim in the lake water by flapping their wings
In the form of swan, duck, and conch shells.
Sometimes my poems are in the form of crows kites and eagles
Sitting jointly on the top branch of the very old banyan or the horse tree.

15.

MayBe

Daily we use to sit on opposite sits face to face
While traveling by the first Shantipur local.
Maybe her name will be Ranjana or Kalpana
Either Anjana, Chandana, or maybe Bndana.
All the names are not bad at all.
Maybe she has two deep eyes and her dense black hairs
Where the darkness of night got thickened may be.
Her face is in the shape of a betel leaf
May raise small wavy in the deep of my mind.
She got down in the Sealdah station,
I am also on my way to the known way as usual.
It is still in the dark if I met her on a half-dark evening.
Only for this, I could not become a poet.
It is not any imaginary step when I step on the
The cemented platform of Sealdah station.
I return to the harsh reality each morning again and again.
Maybe it so happens that I shall have to come back again
As a common man.

16.

The story Of An Eagle

Today listen to the story of an eagle,
The eagle comes daily on time in every morning.
Oh, bird you fly in the distant blue sky far away from the land.
Your chirping is full of cruelty and your wings are rough and tough
Your beck is like a sharp knife.
When we see your eagle-eyed keen-sighted the human being
Cannot remember any art. separately
In the full sunlight on the lamp post on the road
It is just opposite the balcony don't know what urgent work the bird has.
We heard that you are a pet to the Arab Sheiks
What a weird fancy aristocratic strange hobby is this.
Your fury eyes create chest pain.
We are not like the emperors or kings we are. not that renowned
I am a simple common man you are a unique bird although I wait for you.
Count eagerly every second to see you.
You come and sit for some time on the top of the lamp post
After the time is over you fly flapping wings directionless in the far blue.
Every morning I wait eagerly when the bird shall arrive,
For the last few days that gray color red-eyed bird is not coming
I alone wait and count the seconds to see the bird again.

17.

My address

My address is written in the limitless horizon
My address is known to the blue sky spread above.
You can listen to my address uproar with the
The flow of the abundant river.
My address is the chirp of seasonal birds
In philharmonic tune.
You may get my address to the Liege tree
In the deep forest.
Even if you don't get then you can definitely get
My address to the storm.
You may get my address on the mountaintop.
If you don't get it anywhere then definitely
You will get my address to the roaring of the ocean.

18.

The story of an early morning

When returning from my lively city Kolkata almost after a month
On the way to return by Howrah Mumbai Express in the early morning
I was standing on the platform of the old VT station presently known as CST.
To catch the Vashi local of harbor line.
Seen a local train and from the boogie coming out waves of blackheads
As if a tide falls out on the station platform.
Of the busiest city of possibilities Mumbai.
I have seen nobody walking all are running
Maybe their destination is an office nearby, some factory mill, or somewhere else.
There is no sign of tiredness on the faces was there.
The majority of them were from some other state of our country.
Really the taste of business is an indifferent feeling
That helps to live with satisfaction.
I think deeply that my own city Kolkata also has a similar golden past
Why has this disaster of present unemployment miserably gone up?
Tell me when Kolkata will see such a morning
I imagine the dream of a morning like this.
You also see the dream of that golden day which is not at all foggy or a nightmare.
It is the absolute reality oh my lovely affectionate city of Kolkata.
I shall write the story of that shining morning standing on
The platform of Howrah or the Sealdah station in the tide of mass.

19.

What is my destination

Could you come to know what is my destination?
Do you know from where I have started and where is the end?
Do you know from where you have come from
And what is your destination?
In between this, there is only roaming in the sphere puzzle.
AL through the life roaming in search of an unknown treasure.
The trace of the treasure some people get and some aren't
Some people have not even attempted to search for it.
Maybe that will be that snake gem.
Although you have to roam only there is no way to escape
If you have in the way of this life
All through life only search for the address of the destination.
In search of the address roam from zero to the infinity
And hawking for the unknown destination.

20.

One Full Ocean

In the wish to write one ocean, I came out of home
In the addiction to writing. poems.
In the wish to write one ocean, I fly like a bird all over the sky.
In the wish to write about one ocean, I walk along the bank of the river again and again.
In the wish to write one ocean, I put a tent on the hilltop.
In the wish to write about one ocean, I roam around the world.
In the wish to write one ocean with my eager eyes to the watery black cloud.
In the wish to write one ocean, I see daydreaming in deep sleep
On paddy field and mustard field.
In the smell of the greenery, I lose my sense and forget that I have to write one ocean.
I thought I shall write one ocean but could not write one page even.
My wish is not fulfilled although I shall write one ocean at the right time.

21.

Bird You Come

Oh, unknown bird of the morning you come.
I shall synchronize my tune with you in my half-sleep.
It may be rough and loud
Even though try to match with you bird.
Maybe the tune. disturb others or good to listen.
Have you ever touched the sky up above
Or attempted to touch the sky ever.
Like the poet Madhusudan Dutt through the gap of the broken windows
Who wished to touch the sky maybe he could up to his limit.
He wished to be Milton, Shelly, Keats, or maybe Byron
Still living as poet Madhusudan who is not a poet only,
He is a scholar of scholars.
Oh bird you come today and we remind
The unsatisfied soul of Poet Madhusudan
Of our golden past once again.

22.

Sweetheart

In the idle hours, I'm sitting to write a letter oh my sweetheart
To write my own stories which are from the core of my mind.
There was paper and a pen with ink was also there.
Still, I think & search for the word to write for you, my sweetheart.
I deeply think and look at the unlimited blue sky
And wove the net of dreams in my subconscious mind.
My mind goes back far away to the greenery of the field
When you used to pick up mangoes,
After the northwestern storm in the late evening of summer.
My restless youth passed with that field and the
Sweet evenings still knock on the doors of the deep of my heart.
Sill the pen stops repeatedly.
Oh my sweetheart you tell me what shall I write to you?

23.

I'm A Vagabond

Time and again I have gone too far away
I'm a vagabond who went from the East to west direction
Via north and sometimes to the south also.
I have gone too far to Saudi Arabia in the middle east
Also, I have gone to the Bank of the Ocean n of the Persian Gulf
One of the epicenters of art & culture with a glittering past very far Iran.
Again I have gone farther to Sudan
In the core desert of the Sahara In the continent of North Africa.
Even though you call me with your affectionate attraction oh my own city.
Time and again I come back to your peaceful lap free from all tensions.
I take a deep breath in your pure air as I was hungry for a long time.
Oh, my sweet city your sky and the air are still tuned as I saw you in the past.
But still, I feel with the flow of time the memories are lost every day
Under the so-called development where the greeneries are destroyed
By The multi-storied housing complexes.
The ponds & lakes have also vanished in the tide of new developments.
As and when I think to open the closed door of my mind
Every time I found I lost the key to open the closed door of my core heart
And I go out again setting a new direction from far to farther far
I'm still a vagabond today.

24.

The Unseen Love

You are my unseen and untouched indifferent feelings
Although you touch my mind without touch.
You are a splendid feeling oh my love,
And the direction of the tide of my intense love.
I have portrayed you by the color of my imagination
In the deep of my heart.
Overcoming all the resistance and prohibition
I proceed forward.
Do you also think similarly when you are alone in dreamland?
I met you at the peak of the foamy waves
Of the deep Atlantic Ocean in my mind.
And in the dangerous & thrilling undercurrent of the river Brahmaputra.
Or in the midst of a destructive and terrible typhoon that crushes the creation.
You are only my unsmelt charming love of my sweet dreams.
Have you ever felt any touch of my love in your deep sleep
Or when you are in sudden drowsiness from tiredness.

25.

On The Beach Of Life

I love the lively flow of life in the same way
I am afraid of listening to the call of the
Footsteps of the absolute end.
In the ocean of life, the game of creation & destruction is spontaneous.
When the unfathomable water of the Ocean meets the horizon
And the Ocen waves play around.
We all know that water is life so life will be pure
When the holy water mixed with the soil of the earth.
We all love life and are afraid of the call of death
From the abyssal of water all day and night.
And on the sea beach life only paint the motion picture
The roar of fierce death vanishes in the infinity of the sky.
In between ocean water flows with lifestyle
And the mind is worried when at the particular moment
The call will come to mix with the deep Ocean forever.
Requesting you oh death please take rest for a while
Let me draw a handful of paintings of sorrow and happiness of lively life
In the termination of life & death
On the canvas far away between the limit and infinite

26.

It's Lost

Those days with the smell of mango & jack fruit
Those used to make drunk are lost, are lost forever.
Those days with the tase of the pulley on the back
Which used to make us happy with little demand are lost.
Those days with an unknown destination of traveling
Without tickets and get loss are lost.
Those days of distribution of sadness and happiness
Tear and smile with others and the colorful emotional days
Of exchange of mind are lost.
Those days of argument creating a storm in a teacup are lost.
Those days of promotion to higher class in the school
Those obsession days with the smell of the brand-new books are lost.
Those days of little demand and full of excitement
With enormous happiness are lost.
Many things are lost below the bush of bricks, wood, stones, and concrete.
Only those golden days still glitter as happy memories in the mind camera.
Humanity is today from gasping breath inside the neat and clean
Well-arranged limit of housing complexes.

27.
Oh Wind You

Oh, wind don't sing the song of upset again.
Look at how the sky sheds only a stream of happiness.
The cloud shed rain stream
Which is the stream of joy and happiness.
The bright sun after the rain blooms flower
Which is the symbol of love in life.
So wind please don't sing the song of sadness.
Sun you are the king of the day,
Sound the conch in the daylight.
Let life run on its own trend
And this earth be full of rhythm.
On both sides of the river of life
Creation &destruction let go on.
Let the human-race float in the boat of magical tune.
Life knows only to live and move ahead in the flow of happiness.
Oh wind you don't sing the song of upset,
Life knows the real story & the secret to live.

28.

My Sky

I let opened my sky this early morning for you
Oh, my darling my sweetheart you my love.
All of a sudden I saw a flock of white cranes
Are flying on my two-eyed lap.
They are carrying your news flying
In the unlimited blue sky.
The white clouds are also ashamed of them
The milky white flock of birds is flying
Of their own in the blue sky far away.
I also think of myself alone can I not also fly
With the flock of birds and float with them?

29.

One Lump Of Clay & The God

For this season aii the major worship finished
Ganapati, Durga, Kali ,Jagadhatri all'
Some more still there may be.
On the way, I saw that day an artist idolater rubbing
A lump of clay by his feet.
After a few days, the lump of clay will take
The shape of a god or goddess or carriage idol.
By the magical touch of the artist
The lump of clay will take the shape of an idol.
People will worship the idol as God.
The artist idolater will also bow his head
Under the feet of his creation,
When his creation takes the form of God from art,
One day this art was rubbed under the feet of the artist
As a lump of clay only.

30.

Still Flows The Ganges

Oh, Ganges still you are flowing quiet and silent,
Bhagiratha brought you across the sea
He freed all his forefather's souls.
Who were kept as prisoners in the hermitage of Sage Kapil,
They were burnt to charcoals by his furious anger.
This is a story of mythology written in history.
Oh Mother Jhanavi Bhagiratha brought you
From the matted hair of Mahadeva in the ascetic's bowl.
And still today you are flowing the holy mother Gages
Carrying the debris and wastes with you.
Bhagiratha brought your mother to the earth.
For that reason, you are famous as Bhagirathi also.
You mother Ganges.
After that Bhagiratha lost in the down memory lane
The history only knows.
Only mother Ganges you are flowing from north to east,
Maybe you are flowing in search of Bhagiratha's way
Of unknown direction the successor of king Sagar.
That stream is till flows with current.
On the way to your flow the human civilization
Made you polluted time and again.
Oh mother you pardoned them who polluted you
For the sake of development with
Dense motherly affection in your holy lap.
You are the daughter of Himalaya source from Gomukh,
Born and brought up in the mountain Himalayas.
In Hardwar you noble as har ki pouri oh mother.
In the dawn when Sun sets in the late evening

Today also the conch sound echoing
On the bank of the holy mother Ganges. with prayer. and ritual.
In that Triveni Sangam is the place of your union
With river Yamuna and Saraswati.
Still you are flowing quietly oh touchy mother silently.

31.

In The Lap of Cloud

In the lap of clouds, there is no sun this morning.
Black clouds covered all over the sky.
Lightning sparks as if it is whipping frequently
Penetrating the heart of the deep black cloud.
The lightning roars and the earth shakes time and again.
The chill wind blows sounding a thousand sirens. across the horizon.
Along with rain falls cats and dogs by cloud bursting.
Like Pandavas are on the battlefield of Kurukshetra.
All the fields and ponds lakes rivers are flooding.
What a destructive form of the earth today.
After some time the rain stopped the sound of lightning also no more.
Listening to no noise only stunned all around wind also calm and
The rivers, lakes, and ponds are quiet.
As if the earth is back from a journey of infinity.

32.

One Day We Have To Go

One day we all have to go with a smile
Where all the roads reach.
Have to be mixed with the earth
Under or above the feet land.
Life long I roamed from the narrow lanes
To roads and highways and far distances.
Walked a long way in my own country and abroad
Behind that walk, so many reasons were there.
Sometimes I felt tired and taken rest for a while
By the roadside.
Today I have no energy maybe it happens for all
At the fag end of the day when the Sun sets.
Nowadays feel heavy by aging.
Only to look at where all the roads reach.
From the west to the north via east & south
I traveled a long way all my life long for so many reasons.
Now waiting for that day when I have to go with a smile.

33.

We Two

Only some days before we were neighbors,
We were residing in adjacent houses in the same city.
Almost regularly your pet cat used to steal
In our favorite kitchen.
Our pet ducks used to cross your lawn in the flock
Towards the pond nearby our house.
The number of ripe mangoes fallen on our lawn
From your mango tree most often.
That was our household for seven decades
The house was well arranged in all respect.
I used to speak with you only in our eye signals.
Couldn't speak with anytime with you. Alone.
This is a very old story from down memory lane.
This is a painful chapter of Kalakopa village
Of Kashimpur town in Dhaka city.
In between time flew like water through
The rivers Ganges, Padma, and Ichamati.
Still, you are in the same country and losing
Everything I am a refugee now in this country
And still, I am roaming losing the direction and aim.

34.

Torn Documents

Don't know why the down memory lane
Calls me from the past.
That lane knows only to create emotion
Memories of happy moments are also there.
Agree that happiness was little lasting and momentary.
At present those memories are mere past tense only.
Memories are hiding like the stars at night.
Like all the stars are hidden in the depth of the daylight.,
When the Sun rises enlightens the East.
I was surprised again and again thinking about all these puzzles,
My all memories today are simply torn documents only.

35.

Looking Behind

As I look behind my past pulls me back.
The past is now in the deep dark today
And it is full of mistakes.
Whether all my deeds were wrong?
I want to justify it now.
Keep in mind that one day
Today's present also will change to past,
By the call of the future.
All mistakes cannot be corrected
Along the stream of the time river.
The present is ongoing
And the future is on the opposite bank.
You have to go-ahead
You have to float with the flowing stream of time,
You should have to float with the current of the river of life.

36.

Still living

This is an unbelievable feeling that I am alive,
Every morning I woke up on time and sleep on time.
Surviving is feeling like an addiction.
That addiction kept life always busy & speedy.
Surviving is the best blessing of the almighty,
Although only surviving without any target has no use.
It is better to live a short successful life rather than
Living a long life without positive acts.
Sacrifice thyself for the cause of humanity
Is the absolute success and achievement in a lifetime,
By the invisible signal of the Almighty.
So surviving is a success only when you will
Alive in the memory and mind of the mass.

37.

I Wish

I wish I go a thousand years back.
When life was simple and easy
Showmanship had no meaning then.
Every person believed each other in faith.
There was no differentiation in between them.
They were ready to sacrifice for the
Cause of others.without any hesitation.
I wish I shall go back below
The tick wood and sandalwood tree
Where the lion, tiger, bison, and deer
Play freely in the open forest.
Peacock dances with a distended tail feather
To the music and tune of the flute.
Forgetting all the differentiation, the hatred
And the scuffle I wish I go behind
A thousand years back.

38.
Foolish Mind

Oh, my mind is too foolish, have no direction
And absent-minded still I don't know
Why it doesn't understand at all who is of its own
And who is not known?
Betrayed several times by believing others and hurt as well
So I think really am I so ill-fated?
By repeatedly cheating I got a crack in my faith.
They hurt me by scratching and biting,
But I never insulted them to my knowledge.
My power of endurance increased by their repeated hit even injured.
And those who hurt me are disheartened and have gone far away.

39.

Reckon up

Sometimes there is profit and sometimes loss
Sometimes owed sometimes debt
When reconciling the accounts of life.
There is no reconciliation of sacrifice & endurance.
Even if all the accounts can not be reconciled.
Donation can't be measured in the tune of reciprocation.
Love can not be measured in the tune of giving and taking.
Affection also can never be accounted for.
Who will return that account and when.
Who could return the debt of love?
Which donor reconciled his donation as deposited treasure.
Is anybody reconciled at the fag-end of his life
In the late evening?
The conclusion is only zero and the reckoning is zero only.

40.

Don't Say Bye

Don't say no from the core of your heart,
Sure we shall meet again sometime
Maybe somewhere. we can recall each other
Maybe as an unknown,
Although we must meet again,
So don't say bye.
There is nothing called an end
Where there is an end there budding
The expression to start with.
The flower drops and from that flower grows seed
From seed plant & from plant flower blooms again
This means the flow of evolution.
So there is nothing like the end.
When the tune of the end rings up with that echo
Rings up the morning tune of flute for the Renaissance.
So please don't say bye shall meet sure somewhere..
If you can remember your previous birth
Then everything will be brightened in your memory
And the forgotten past shall glitter & shining.

41.

Oh Wind You

Oh, wind don't sing the song of upset again.
Look at how the sky sheds only a stream of happiness.
The cloud shed rain stream
Which is the stream of joy and happiness.
The bright sun after the rain blooms flower
Which is the symbol of love in life.
So wind please don't sing the song of sadness.
Sun you are the king of the day,
Sound the conch in the daylight.
Let life run on its own trend
And this earth be full of rhythm.
On both sides of the river of life
Creation &destruction let go on.
Let the human-race float in the boat of magical tune.
Life knows only to live and move ahead in the flow of happiness.
Oh wind you don't sing the song of upset,
Life knows the real story & the secret to live.

42.

Nothing Is There

No grass is there in the field,
No leaves are there in the trees,
No cloud was seen in the blue sky above.
No wind is blowing
And the Sun is not having its brightness.
No motion in life,
No water in the river
Honesty is no more there.
The face is lost behind the mask.
The rainwater is the eyewater of weeping,
People are crying you console them.

43.

Still we speak

Still, we speak sometimes alone
And sometimes absent-minded,
Whispering with my unrest youth.
When I go back to my past time
Along the mud way in the paddy field
With greeneries all around.
I can feel the sweet melodious tune
Of the cuckoo when I walk through
Down memory lane in the Wind of spring season.
Remind me of that discolored yellow
Days of youthful youth.
When nothing was an impossible task.
I still remind those days when my
My mind melts like a candle in love
And whispers with me when alone.
I tell everything to the princess of
My dream with my utmost love feelings and affection.
And then I ride on the ups and downs of time.
I walk through again and again and come back
Again in the hard reality.
I wake up from drowsiness
The Sun rises in the transparent blue sky
In the east and glitters with its full brightness.

44.

Water Picture

That water picture is the motion picture of life.
The water picture gets alive by the scratches
Of artist's brush.
And the poet writes his feelings with pen and ink
In the manuscript from the deep of his heart
Is also a water picture.
That's the reason people call him an absent-minded poet.
The art drawn by the artist put up for auction
The price of those valuable arts goes up & down.
The poem written by the poets some times published
Sometimes not although the water picture of poems
Written by the poet will be alive forever & evergreen.
In the mind of people and the core of the mind of the poet.
Although a maximum of them flies like torn-out leave to infinity.
Even the poet doesn't stop writing the water picture of poems.
That's the reason the poet doesn't know to stop in defeat
He writes the poem of life in pen & ink
In the form of water picture ever alive.

45.

In Far Abroad

For quite a few years I am in far abroad
I came to this foreign land in search of
A golden future.
I am an expatriate now detached from you
Oh my affectionate love only mine nearest one
My hidden happiness you my city of love.
I am compelled to detach from you
By destiny and the ups and downs of life
I have compromised with the situation.
My mind never agreed with that compromise
Today I am a successful man in my career
I reached the peak of my targeted improvement
Although in every footstep I get the touch of
The wind smells of your soil oh my only love
Oh, my own city of affection only you.

46.
Still living

This is an unbelievable feeling that I am alive,
Every morning I woke up on time and sleep in time.
Surviving is a feeling like an addiction.
That addiction kept life always busy & speedy.
Surviving is the best blessing of the almighty,
Although only surviving without any target has no use.
It is better to live a short successful life rather than
Living a long life without positive acts.
Sacrifice thyself for the cause of humanity
Is the absolute success and achievement in a lifetime,
By the invisible signal of the Almighty.
So surviving is a success only when you will
Alive in the memory and mind of the mass.

47.

The Life Circle

Nowadays, no pond or lake is visible wherever you see in the city.
Only the massive high rise. residential complexes are there.
In our locality, there is a medium pond whose water
Is crystal transparent. till today.
I was sitting on one side of that pond in the late evening. one day
After a long period, I sat alone from my busy schedule
On the cemented step of that pond.
All of a sudden a small piece of brick fell into the water
First, it stirred the water and then made a tiny circle
Then the circle slowly bigger and bigger and then vanish.
It reminded me of the deep philosophy of life in my subconscious mind.
In the life Ocean also few incidents suddenly strike and stir.
Then comes evolution similar to the circle.
Life spindles like a circle in the center of the circle I am alone.
The circle vanishes in its own time I'm only sitting in surprise

48.

My Dream

I have forgotten to see dreams nowadays.
In my childhood, I saw a lot of dreams
Hearing stories from grandmother
I had also a dream. princess with
Long curly dense black hair like cloud.
A lot of stories heard about swimming
In the Ocean of milk & of Nilkamal
And his brother Lalkamal.
Also the story of the demoness
Who dominoes the palace of sleeping,
And I saw in my childhood dream
I am flying on a horse with wing
In the midst of the thick cloud by awakening
The sleeping princess with me towards
An unknown direction & destination.

49.

The Lost Youth

Looking at the south direction of the sky
The half-moon is still visible in this early morning.
The half-moon has an innocent smile
Like a toothless old woman.
Not a single star is visible in this morning's sky.
Now spring season is in full swing.
In this dark early morning of peak spring
The Cuckoo is calling with its
Sweet melodious and magical tune. Frequently.
The bird is announcing that spring has arrived.
And the silk cotton & the flame flower tree
Spreads red color on the far horizon
Their new leaves are growing which is
The symbol that the spring season is ongoing.
The spring season will be for some more days
As time doesn't know to stop and time never stops
On its own, the spring season also shall pass away
A few days after that f moon with lost youth will
Also, set in the deep dark of the new moon.
Again the moon shall rise with a new form
From the lost youth to the Bloom of Youth
And shall spread its soft pleasant magical light.
As if it will pour honey on the sky and earth
I and the whole world shall astonish
By that charming heavenly scene.

50.

Looking At The Road

For whom I look at the road,
He has deceived me today.
I have exchanged minds keeping a hand in hand
He gave me word only to fool me.
He has gone too far away abroad
Now I only count the days is my destiny.
He used to write very attractive letters
And I also replied to those letters with a lot of hope.
Now he doesn't write of dreams of hope.
I can also wait no more
Only I can wait and have nothing to do
Someone, please say me what shall I do.

51.

May Be Again

Maybe again we will meet,
Maybe not at all in this life
Maybe we will meet after rebirth.
Maybe meet with the beautiful country
Full of greeneries and the melodious tunes of birds
My dearest one oh my own magical country.
In this life, I am an expatriate,
Gone too far away another country.
Although when I am alone and look at the lonely sky
Or when I listen to the silent cry of the wind
I feel again& again that I should go back to
The lap of my own motherland full of
Evergreen affection and love are where I feel my pulse.
Still, I can not reach you my sweetest motherland
As to fulfill my dreams of high hopes
I am settled already in this foreign land.
That is the cause I think again I shall meet you
After my rebirth may be in some auspicious moment.

52.

In Life & In The War

Music, tune, and rhythm you are in the war
And also you are the inspiration of life.
Music, tune, and rhythm you are in love and happiness
And you are in separation and distress also.
Music, tune, and rhythm you are in hope
And you are in despair also.
Music, tune, and rhythm you are in sacrifice
And you are in enjoyment also.
Music, tune, and rhythm you are in religion
And you are in an atheist also.
Music, tune, and rhythm you are in the faith
And you are in disbelief also.
You all are in joy and sorrow.
You all are with the winner and the conquered also.
Only you can not be other than the bud of the creation.

53.

From An Expatriate

While sitting alone abroad and eagerly waiting for
The letter carrying the news from my motherland.
Almost every day I wrote letters in tons and send them by the wind
And I have taken a long breadth equal to one full sky.
Now when is the time after a long waiting to return
To you has come oh my motherland this charming magical city
Calls me from behind, again and again, attracting and giving signals
With her prosperity and charming beauty.
I fixed my mind that this will be the last time to get something more.
Even though I couldn't return to your greeneries oh my motherland
Oh, my country where I cherished my childhood and left it.
I have sold myself to this country of opportunity & prosperity. Here.
I couldn't return to your shelter full of peace and safe and happiness.
So again I am writing this letter to you with eagerness like the mountain high
And maybe again I have to take a long breadth equal to one full sky.

54.

My Sky

Oh, my sky I open it this morning for you.
A flock of white cranes flew
As if in my two eye corners.
They are the bearers of your message flying
And floating in the unlimited blue sky.
The white clouds are also quite ashamed
To those flock of white cranes.
See how that milky white flock is flying
In the very far blue sky.
I also dream in my mind and think,
That can I not float in that flock like a bird?

55.

The Tradition

Stereotype this life starts from the lower primary class
After passing out from high school go to college life
Some after graduation do a post-graduate or research scholarship,
Then starts a good service or in the teaching profession.
This is the stereotype and normal rhythm of life like a
Good looking tambourine and its name is Life.
A few of them do something different against the normal flow
In the urge for survival in the lifestream.
Life flows in its own motion sometimes very calm and quiet
And sometimes storm fall out on the bank of life river.
In this way in the spring of youth with a touch of love
Some listen to the magical chirping of affection
Whear few succeeded and few fail in the love game.
Even though lots of them lead a family life and some are separated.
Then the life flows stereotype only to fulfill
The commitments and responsibilities its called life.
Life has a motion one day comes the long waited
And unwanted that day of farewell.
As if the Sun sets at dawn in the early evening.
After that wait for the uninvited last moment
And too long retirement with ever ended waiting.
I am waiting with an empty vision just like a neglected character
In the drama stage,
The drop scene has fallen in its own time.
All the spectators slowly left one by one from the theater hall,
Only I feel totally lonely and I don't know when loneliness swallows me
Still, as the show goes on there will never be last night for this drama.
The tradition of the flow of life continues and its name is life.

56.

Fulfilment Of Wish

I was a mere teacher only a companion
To guide you in the starting hour of your life.
Although my mind did not obey
I exchanged my mind to you.
I never expressed my love to you
But you also couldn't feel the desire of the eye
Or by the light wishful touches?
Maybe you also but you also didn't express it.
All those chapters are closed today.
Few days before you complete the postgraduate
From the University.
That day your father came to invite me with
The invitation card for your marriage.
So many times he requested me to be present
In the occasion.
I believe that you will not be happy still
I pray for your happy married life.
Even though you make your happy nestle
With another person.
And let our wish shall not be fulfilled for this life.

57.

Wavy

Oh my dear sweet city of joy wavy and the lovely city I have ever seen
You are my very own wavy city oh my love.
Number of waves of mass movements, and processions flow through your
Lanes and by lanes time and again.
And in fields & grounds holds mass meetings and fairs.
Sometimes in the Brigade parade ground orI in the Red Road
And sometimes below the Monument.
The mass wave moves through your sorely wounded heart.
By the intoxication of movement, they forget that you are also now aged one
Your age is now over three hundred years since the time of Jobcharnak.
You are the silent witness of bloodsheded struggles.
Still can remember after the independence the soil of Dharmatala turned red
By the blood of the martyr of the food movement and also
The youth movement of Sevetyone was devastating.
After those also the river Ganges flows silently.
But the resonance of those movements is still there today also.
At the same time Victoria Memorial, Millennium Park & Babur ghat
Are the witness of a number of love affairs and promises
Maximum of those are spoiled at the budding stage
And few of them are just merely plays of love only.
Long live oh my wavy city with the ever-green youth
Of a sweet naughty girl with charm and greenery
You are the inspiration of dreams and imaginations of the whimsical poet,
Still, you are flowing in your own graceful rhythm and tune,
The tradition rolls on as usual with the change of time.

58.

The Face & The Mask

If there is a face then definitely there shall be the mask,
The mask covers the face
Is known to the human civilization.
It is not worth wearing a mask always.
The masked face keeps on fooling me almost daily.
Sometimes they act unfaithful,
The same face act as a more reliable one when getting the chance.
They create confusion and doubt for simple-minded people.
When they understand the matter there is no way to repent only.
If the mask falls down it is almost impossible to show the face.
It is very easy to give tons of excuses for wearing the mask
How effective are you proving with your naked face?

59.

The Unknown Bird

The unknown bird is captive
Inside the body cage.
The bird is tied with
The chain of magical affection.
Another bird is pulling secretly
The reel winded with the thread of affection.
It is the mind bird that stays in the deep of the heart.
When that invisible affection tread shall get pulled
The unknown bird will vanish where
When who knows?

60.

Remember All Those Days

Remember all those days of dawn in the late evening
With light darkness and soiled with dust.
Remember all those days of games to break and to build,
In the fair and in the magic of idle days.
Remember all those days when the mornings were busy
And it was a preparation to run in a hurry.
Remember all those days. we could fall in love
To whom we look in affection momentarily.
Remember all those days when the difference of
Good and bad were merely meaningless.
Remember all those days we felt the urge to go ahead
Hurriedly in life without any reason.
Remember all those days when life meant
A race run run and only to run.
And all the other things were meaningless only.
Remember all those days when the song of Palanquin
And all those days were full of colorful dreams.

61.

When The Eagle Cries

In the northeast when we see the vermilion cloud
And when the flow of wind stops,
All of a sudden strong wind blows all around in the four directions.
All the corners shaking the horizon.
A thousand sirens whistle & sounds time and again all around.
The chicks of the eagle also wept with tears,
When the eagle cries.
Numbers of thunders frequently shake nature.
The earth and creature vibrate,
The heart of the cruel eagle also shakes
The eagle doesn't know where to go back again.
His nest no more exists as the wind blows in speed.
The eagle cries silently in the turbulent wind
And the splash of water.
The lighting vibrates all along the horizon
Like the king of dancers, Shiva shakes his long hairs
And he sounds his damru in one hand,
On the other hand, moves his trident emitting fireballs.
His anger light emits from his third eye guiding
The direction of moksha in the Milkyway along the distant sky.
The thunder strikes the earth again and again
The sky is kissing the earth on her soft leaps with fiery love
Wrapping the earth all around with the mad drunken wind
The creation of new life will be bloomed in this
Affectionate love of the sky, wind, and the earth & nature
When the eagle cries.

62.

The Touch

When it rains cats and dogs
When everybody stays inside
Or search for shelter from the rain.
That man gets wet in the rain
Till the rain stops.
Two years before when the whole world.
Was stirred up by the fury of the Corona epidemic
Then the epidemic attacked that man's
Three-member family also.
All of them were admitted to the hospital.
The man survived and returned to his home
Leaving his wife & the little daughter forever.
So when it rains may be drizzling or in cats and dogs
That man feels the touch of his lost dears
Who have vanished in the too-far blue sky.
That man takes their sweet smell in his deep breadth
From the rain the smell of his wife and daughter
Till the rain stops and gets refreshed with the smell.

63.

The Black Hole

One day you, me all will vanish and be untraceable
In the deep dense darkness of the black hole
Where the ray also not permitted to enter
Dense darkness exists only.
Before disappearing into the black hole
It doesn't happen by the fury of a long breath
Of the people you take watery grave
In the Abyssal Sea of Oblivion.
You should be cautious about this
Before disappearing into the black hole this society
And your successors don't forget you in hatred.
It is ideally far better to disappear into the black hole
Of the too-far-away sky before the insult and hatred
By society and your near and dear ones.
There should be a minimum touch of faith & transparency
In every single moment & every footstep count of life.

64.

Bye Forever

Another day has arrived on its wing
In this dark early morning.
Sometimes it flitters its wings
And sometimes its face is full of sorrow,
Maybe somebody heartened it.
Sometimes it is unaccounted happy.
This way the day passes sometimes it
Come down on the lawn to meet its hunger.
Then comes the late evening the day came
In the form of a bird again flown back into the darkness
Of the late evening who came in the early morning.
Again it will come back as another new day.
When the dense darkness of the night will disappear
By the rising red Sun will announce the arrival of a new day.
Again it will fly back in the late evening hours
Like this, life will also announce and say bye forever.

65.

The Sound Of Light

Listened to the sound of wind and weeping of the sky
If you try to hear you can in your ear when you are alone.
Light also has sound and light also can speak,
When the stars twinkle in the far sky.
When the light ball runs through the abandoned lake,
When the fireflies penetrate the dense darkness of the silent night,
And sparks frequently in their own wish.
All these are the soundless language of light speaks.
When the thunderclap tore the heart of the sky
All the creation terrifies by the sound of light.
The sound of light speaks then creating an echo all around.
I saw it so many times on my way when alone silent deep dark night
And when crossing the river the light speaks in their own signal
I was surprised by my wide eyes.
That signal sometimes creates fury and sometimes brought happiness.
It hammers the heart in humans with the support of nature.

66.

Be Warned

The vultures are still there today in disguise
Be warned and be aware of the destination of life.
The holy war of Kurukshetra was won by the truth,
The pride and injustice were defeated.
Offering, belief & discipline was followed
By the Pandavas the great warriors of Mahabharat.
Evil spreads its race growing from its own blood,
Uptill today continuously.
Those disastrous vultures keep the company
To those accumulated sins. through the ages.without rest.
The vultures are still there today
That's why lie fraud, easily attracts people in the way to sin.
To achieve the easy goal they follow the wake of greediness,
Forgetting the difference between good and bad.
Then only the vultures appear as an advisor
Be warned & go ahead on the road of life and be awakened.
Proceed forward on the way of life with caution,
Identify the vultures
Otherwise, ruin is assured on the way to religion.

67.
The Incident

Today the incident stirring the society
Brings a radical change with a new wave.
Society starts with a fresh new page in history,
With the flow of time the same incident
Is treated as a rumor only and is simply a false story.
Today the incident spread as true
In the future, the same story proves false only.
Even though the truth speaks out.
False incidents mislead people for a few days and time.
And when it harms the interest of the individual
The same false incident speaks about reality.
In the course of time, the same person says
The incident didn't happen at all with a big face.

68.

The Beautiful Time

By the law of the time, everything is past today
Which I own only and I was the owner.
Only a few beautiful time is still with me today
In the balance book as a credit.
The deposit never increases in interest
Although the invested time is more than enough.
That's the reason I tried to distribute it again and again,
A beautiful time for all of you.
So many times I dIstribute that deposit
But it never reduces by the rule of mathematics.
This is like a never-ending story.
Everyone has their own beautiful time
Some understand even a maximum of them are not aware.
You also distribute your own beautiful time,
Then only you can feel that your capital of beautiful time
Never finish ii is the same as it was.
You will enjoy unlimited satisfaction
Distributing the never-ending capital of beautiful life.

69.

Today In The Sky

Today the sky is fair of white clouds,
There are colorful shows in the sky.
I pass the morning time sitting
\On the boat of clouds.
My mind is floating and rowing
By sitting & rowing on the cloud's lap.
It travels to that unknown palace
Of the fairy tells told by the grandma,
And where the two prince brothers
Play with their swords.
In that dream country
The birds also speak in musical tunes.
Only the dream princess with golden color
Floats in her wept water.
I think only when I shall meet the princess
And bring her from the unknown palace
Through the milky river, of white clouds flying
On a white horse with wings.

70.

Mixed Up

The memories are of mine and of yours'
Memories are of smiling and weeping both.
Those days of the memories of both of us
All mixed up and synchronize in the same tune
In both of our minds.
The story is of happiness and sadness as well,
All the memories and the stories fly together
Sometimes the mind is careless and sometimes lively..
Sometimes swallowed by umpteen silence.
All the memories and stories for both of us
Mixed up together.
This is the absolute truth and free drama stage of life.
The unlimited number of shows held at this stage
All the dramas are full of magical family stories
In which all the memories of
Smile and sorrow all mixed up together..

71.

Night Full Of Dream

A time was there when I was eager to see your sweet smile
And I was ready to do any impossible task spontaneously
When you just expressed your wish.
I used to see dreams for a full night and I dreamt of you.
When you told me that you need to have the mango from the tree
I used to ride the three immediately to have it and give the mango to you.
You only tell me whenever I felt nervous?
No no no never.
You just listen to the lizard sounds three times means it's true, true. and true. Only.
That's the reason I dreamt of you for a full night you also might be for me of your own.
A few days before we went to the seabeach nobody was with us on we two were there.
The beach was also lonely exactly as I see you daily in the dream for full night.
Then the Sun was ready to set it was late evening your
fancy slippers were swept away by the sea wave and you were worried,
I ran to get the slippers and you were all alone there on the beach.
I could bring your fancy slippers of your choice only you were missing.
Seeing you alone few human animals kidnapped you behind the nearest bush
They kept your lifeless body and I lost you forever with the setting Sun. of late evening.
Believe me, since that day I can not do anything
And I forget to see a night full of dreams.

72.

The Endless

The Ocean of life flows in the direction
On the way to endless infinity.
Don't know when the walk started on the road
That road was also lost and wiped off & smoky today.
Even though it is unknown we have to go ahead.
This is life and the Ocean of life knows to move only.
So it is the tradition to go ahead in a direction
Without any destination.
Up till today, the Ocean of life flows
Sometimes it's slow and sometimes fast.
It never stops for a moment even.
In this endless voyage sometimes
Life loudly laughs and dances by clapping in rhythm,
Sometimes drown in deep thinking when affectionate.
Everything ends when life lands on reality.
Although life has to proceed onwards
Towards the direction of infinity
Which is endless and unknown.

73.

The Girl

When the sky covers by deep black watery clouds
The girl comes out of her home on the lane.
She comes out like this when the northeastern sky
Is covered by dense black clouds.
Then she slowly walks on the road in the rain.
I could never understand why the girl is doing this,
But on that day it was clear to me the reason behind it.
I was also returning by the same lane and the girl was
Just face to face with me and I saw that the girl is
Weeping and her chin is flooding with water from her eye.
I asked her why she acts like this.
She answered it is very simple otherwise her sorrow shall be open
This is the only way to hide her eyewater behind the rain.
Otherwise, her wept eyes shall get caught by others.
Later I heard that the poor girl was in love with some boy
But the boy left her forever on midway.
That's why a number of girls still weep in the heavy rain
Under the open sky when being cheated by their loved ones.
As the girl still gets wet with rain to hide her eye water
Till today behind the vision of this selfish society

74.

The Naughty Girl

When I look in the northeast direction,
In the late evening when the blazing midday sun is about to set.
As far as visible I try to see one piece of dense black cloud
In the far away northeast direction. near the horizon.
That is the direction of the naughty girl I am eagerly searching for.
Gradually she will grow up and then she will dance and crush
In between the fury sky and the earth.
Her unruly behavior will shake in all directions.
That is with nonstop heavy rain & strong stormy wind
And destroying everything that comes on her way.
The stormy wind shall bring cool coldness.
Daily I search in the northeast direction for a piece of cloud
But in vain can't find a single piece of cloud full of water
No today also the naughty girl did not come in the form of
Northeastern monsoon shaking all along the horizon,
At the fag end of the day.

75.

In The Forests Of People

I am one of the forests of people
In the rush of day and night.
Every day I float here and there
On the road by bus and train,
And in the lanes and bylanes
Which are full of puzzles.
I can see only people anywhere I look,
Many of them have no direction at all.
I also float with the flow being one of them.
In this forest of people, some are quadruped
And some are carnivorous spineless animals.
I proceed further caution keeping an open eye.
A lot of unknowns can be searched in these forests.
All these are the collections,
What you see in these people's forests daily.

76.

I Come Back Again

I come back again and again
In the door of love, affection is caged with lock & key.
I come back again and again
When I look at the aura of the moon I feel that I lost my vision,
Both my eyes are covered by cataracts.
I come back again and again
I wish to be hardworking but can't be
As I have lost that energy and enthusiasm.
The Society rejects me again and again.
They have no sympathy in their hearts
By listening, nothing is there all around
I can not hear now.
Only there is no affection, no energy, no urge, no vision, no light
Everything is covered by dense black darkness.
Time is standing still like stationery,
Today it seems like time is motionless.
Although I come back again and again.

77.

A Fist Full Of Hope

Every day the red sun rises on the lap of the Ocean
Or from the back of the mountain just like a cool fireball.
The sun jumps in its own direction to the sky likes
A child laughing with his newly grown teeth.
A magical dream and a fistful of hope suddenly wake up
In the universe and the creation.
The same sunburns by its heat wave for the whole day
As life burns every day.
This is the law of nature the earth march around the sun.
Slowly the heat of the sun cools down
Again the sun drowns with a smile like a child while setting
On the lap of the Atlantic Ocean or hiding behind a mountain.
The horizon gets covered by dense dark very slowly.
Again the hide-and-seek game goes on in between dream and hope,
This is a routine game of that restless innocent child.
The red sun every day rises and sets in the same tradition
Even though the hope is still alive.
On the morning of the very next day let all the love & affection
On the earth be alive with a fist full of hope.

78.

My Poem

My poem floats in the lap of the clouds on its wings
In the too-far-blue sky. where the flock of birds takes
Breath of liberation.
My poem plays to the tune of Anklet in the Feet of
The teenage girl.
My poem tells the story to the hard-working people
The tell from the core of their heart.
My poem attacks the exploiter with a breakneck speed
Like a hunter eagle with red eyes and snatches the right
For the absorbed.& exploits.
My poem brings a new wave of hope and renaissance
To the worker, farmer, and the day laborer.
My poem blooms as a flower in this country of sunrise.
My poem tells the words of hope who lost their hope
My poem shows the way of the direction to go ahead
In the own target.
Today my poem has lost direction and don't know where to fly,
I also have lost the way where to go with my poem.

79.

The Flow Of Life

Life flows every day as usual following tradition,
A number of people daily take birth and say bye forever daily.
Although those who are newcomers their addresses
Are already fixed.
But who takes bye forever for which address they left is unknown.
Every day the Sun rises and the Sun sets in the west direction of the sky,
During dawn in the late evening spreads the rosiness in the blue sky
Then rises the moon with a cool aura.
With the soft light in the morning, the moon also vanishes
Oh in the morning you will not see the moon again.
So the route of arrival is fixed always
The way of bye forever along the hazy milky way
In the direction of stars too far away.w
When someone goes there never comes back again
So coming & going is the flow of life
Have to be accepted whatever painful it may be.
The wave rolls on with the flow of life silently
Every moment of it's. own wish.

80.
The Shadow

When you stand in front of the mirror you will see
The image which is transparent doesn't shake.
The same you if stand on the side of a pond
And look at the crystal transparent water,
You will see your image on the water vibrating
In the light breeze.
When you move away from the mirror
Your image vanishes immediately.
And the same thing happens when you move away
From the water pond, you will not get the image.
Only the shadow never leaves you it follows you.
But for you, the importance of shadow
Is always less than the image.
Exactly you don't listen to the advice of a wellwisher
And you blindly believe those so-called nearest friends
Who flatters through your past and present also future.

81.

May Be Or May Not Be

Hope maybe there or may not be,,
But the dream must be there.
Love and affection may be there or may not be,
But futile love must be there.
Peace may be there or may not be,
But the want of peace must be there.
Discipline may be there or may not be,
But disorder must be there.
The light may be there or may not be,
But darkness must be there.
Knowledge may be there or may not be,
But ignorant must be there.
Education may be there or may not be,
But lack of education must be there.
Fulfilness may be there or may not be,
But incompletion must be there.
Achievement is there may or may not be,
But underachievement must be there.
Success is there may or may not be,
But failure must be there.
Tide is there may or may not be,
But ebb must be there.
Only the creation & destruction were there
Exist at present and must be in the future.
As birth & death were there
Exist at present and must be in the future.

82.

When I Repent

When I stand all alone
The light orange sunrays enter through
The open window in the east,
Or the soft sunlight of late evening of the dawn
Floats the balcony of the west.
In that magical moment, I ask to myself
Do you not repent today in your core of mind?
I answer oh yes definitely I repent,
But my soul says what is the use of saying all those,
I say in reply why as you have stepped on
The fag end of the day now?
Don't you wish to look at the backward
The debit credit is the accounting of life.
I say see I am always careless about all those
Now tell me about something else.
Then my inner mind told understand
You are dodging yourself and shall not open your mind.
I say nothing really the whole life passed by dodging only
Done so many things but nothing is finished.
This is the dodging with self.
The sun slowly sets in its own way as usual,
Darkness covers all around all the birds return to their nest.
As if changing the scene of the drama
At the fag end of the day of life I found that I and myself
All mixed up together in one and only one I myself.

83.

The Martyr

I am a martyr from my youth to till death,
For the country, I have sacrificed my life.
In lieu of that, you have honored me
By calling me a martyr which is colored
In my own blood.
In a country of martyrs
Like Khudiram,Bhagat Singh & Rajguru,
I'm also a martyr of revenge
By your narrow political reason.
Every year on this very special day
You sit together to celebrate.
You tell my sacrifice my sufferance
And about my braveries to make me forget my untold pain
The extortioner ruler hurt and severely tortured
And injured me repeatedly.
By the revenge of the ruler,
I lost the key to my dream of happiness.
All my dreams turned to ashes is my only gain today.
And today I am covered by the photo frame
As a silent photo only
In my memory you cover my martyr's dias with garlands,
And my sad memories silently smile looking at you.
The sky trembles and the wind roars to the slogan
You shout in my name and you just try to make me forget
By celebration and posthumous honors.
You celebrate Martyr's day as an announced holiday. today.
Can you not listen to the sad tune of the flute in the wind,
Never You can repay debt for the bloodshed by me the Martyr.

84.

I Shall Come Back Again Translated From Aabar Ashibo Phire Written By Jibananada Das In Bengali

I shall come back again in this Bengal on the bank of Dhanshiri river,
Maybe in the form of a morning crow or in the form of a brahminy kite or shalik.
In this land of celebration of new rice in the month of Kartik.
Floating amidst foggy morning I shall return under the cool shadow of this jackfruit tree.
Maybe in the form of a duck and shall wear in my palmet red feet like the anklet of a young girl.
Shall spend the whole day swimming in the smell of water spinach,
I shall come back again in the attraction of this Bengal's river field and farm
In the sorrowful bank wet by Jalangi's waves.
You may see me where the flies are flying forming whirlwinds in the evening wind,
In the silk cotton tree, you may listen to the white owl chirping
Or an infant is playing with the khai paddy on the lawn.
Maybe a teenage boy is piloting a small boat with a torn-out white rudder in the filthy water of Rupsha,
The white cranes return to their nests flying through the red cloud,
In that crowd, you will get me.
I shall come back again in this Bengal on the bank of Dhanshiri river,

85.

Banalata Sen A Translated Version Written By Jibanananda Das In Bengali

I'm walking for thousand years,
I am travelling on the orbit of this world.
My journey is from the Cylon Sea to the Malayan seas
Through the deep dense midnights.
I travelled a lot in the hazy kingdoms of Ashoka in Bimbisar
I was there far away in the darkness of Bidharbha city.
I am a tired soul around me the frothy sea of life rolling all around.
Solace and consolation were given to me by the lady of Natore
My oasis of love.
Her hairs were age-old Bidisha's midnight grace.
Her face was an artistic sculpture of Shrabasti,
The sailor who lost his destination with the rudder broken in a far-off sea.
A land of green grass when he sees in the Cynamon Island.
Like that, I've seen her in the dark
She told, " Where have you been so long?"
Raising her eyes like the bird's nest Natore's Banalata Sen.
At the end of the day like the sound of dews dawn comes a hawk from its wing
Shakes off the smell of the Sun,
From the earth extinct are all the colours.
The manuscripts then arrange for the writing
Then coloured stories glitter in the form of fireflies.
All the birds return to their nests,
All rivers get ended all the transactions of this life
Stays back only deep dark that only remains
And sit face to face me and Banalata Sen.